Let's Give the Pu

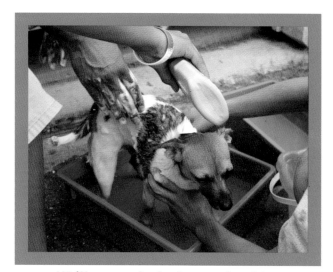

**Written and photographed by
Anjeanetta Prater Matthews**

Here is my new puppy.

She is dirty and needs a bath.

2

My friend came to help me bathe my puppy. First, we filled a lot of buckets with water to get prepared.

We put her in the water, and

my dad helped us soak her.

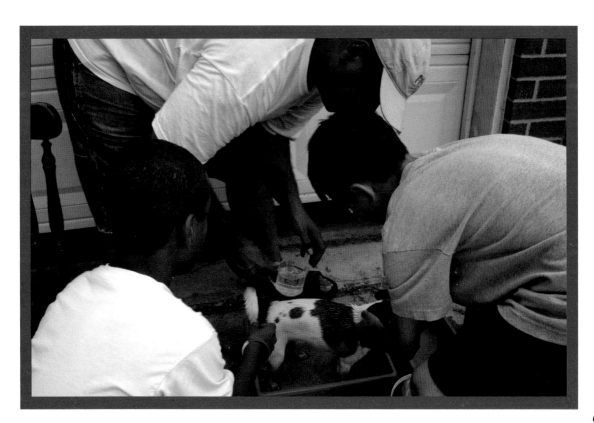

We put a lot of soap on her so she could get really clean. We washed her very well.

After we washed her, we rinsed

her to remove all of the soap.

Then we dried her off with a towel.

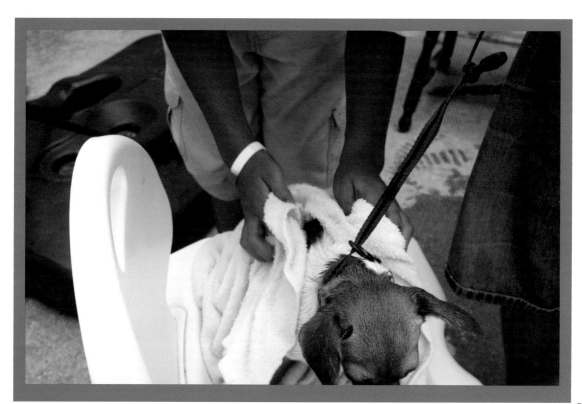

Finally, we put her little jacket on her. My puppy is so clean and cute!

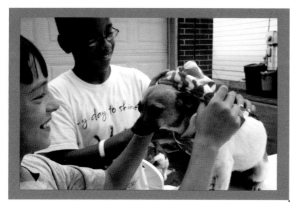